Don't yah Know?
Yah MUST
finish the Race
First!!!

Apostle Bill Amor

"Don't yah Know? Yah MUST finish the Race First!!!"
written by Bill Amor
1st Edition © 2025 by Bill Amor
ISBN: 979-8-9995696-3-9

To purchase all of Apostle Bill's books. Scan this QR Code:

CONTENTS

CONTENTS

Summary of Apostle Bill Amor's New Book: "Don't yah Know? Yah MUST finish the Race First!!!"

Apostle Bill Amor's latest book, *"Don't yah Know? Yah MUST finish the Race First!!!"*, draws deeply from the Amplified Bible (AMP) and centers on the metaphorical race described in **1 Corinthians 9:24**. This scripture emphasizes that all runners compete, but only one receives the prize, urging believers to run their spiritual race with purpose and determination. The book is a motivational guide for Christians, encouraging them to persevere in their faith journey and achieve their ultimate goal of eternal life with God.

Key Themes and Insights

1. The Spiritual Race as a Metaphor for Life

Apostle Amor explores how life is akin to an athletic competition, where discipline, focus, and endurance are essential. Drawing from **1 Corinthians 9:24**, he explains that just as athletes train rigorously to win a physical prize, Christians must dedicate themselves wholeheartedly to their spiritual growth and calling.

2. Running with Purpose

The book emphasizes running "in such a way" to seize the prize, which I interpret as living intentionally according to God's will. I highlight practical steps for believers to align their lives with biblical principles, including prayer, scripture study, and active service within their communities.

3. Overcoming Obstacles

I address common challenges faced by Christians—such as doubt, temptation, and worldly distractions—and provide scriptural strategies for overcoming these hurdles. I remind readers that perseverance is key and that God equips His followers with strength through faith.

4. *The Eternal Prize*

Unlike earthly competitions where only one person wins, I want to underscore that in the spiritual race, every believer who finishes faithfully receives the ultimate reward: eternal life with Christ. Furthermore, I will connect this idea to other scriptures about heavenly rewards (e.g., Philippians 3:14) so as to encourage readers not to lose sight of this eternal perspective.

Writing Style

The book combines theological depth with practical application, making it accessible for both new believers and seasoned Christians. I use anecdotes from my ministry experience alongside biblical exegesis to illustrate the points vividly.

Conclusion

"Don't yah Know? Yah MUST finish the Race First!!!" serves as both an encouragement and a challenge for Christians to remain steadfast in their faith journey. By focusing on discipline, purposefulness, and reliance on God's grace, I want to inspire readers to run their race well and claim the eternal prize promised by Scripture.

The Most Appropriate Chapters for Apostle Bill Amor's Book: "Don't yah Know? Yah MUST finish the Race First!!!"

To structure this book effectively and align it with its central theme of running the spiritual race, the chapters are organized to guide readers step-by-step through understanding, preparing for, and persevering in their faith journey.

Below is a detailed outline of the most appropriate chapters for this book:

Chapter 1: Understanding the Spiritual Race

This chapter introduces the concept of life as a spiritual race, drawing from **1 Corinthians 9:24-27**. It explains the metaphor of running a race as used in Scripture and sets the foundation for why Christians are called to run with purpose. Key topics include:

- The biblical basis for viewing life as a race.

- The importance of recognizing God's calling.

- Differentiating between earthly rewards and eternal prizes.

Chapter 2: Preparing for the Journey

Preparation is essential for any race. This chapter focuses on how believers can spiritually prepare themselves to run well. Drawing from passages like **Ephesians 6:10-18** (the Armor of God), it covers:

- Building a strong relationship with God through prayer and scripture study.

- Equipping oneself with spiritual tools such as faith, righteousness, and truth.

- Developing discipline and self-control as emphasized in **1 Corinthians 9:25.**

Chapter 3: Running with Purpose

This chapter emphasizes intentionality in living out one's faith. Using examples from both Scripture (e.g., **Philippians 3:13-14**) and real-life testimonies, it discusses:

• Setting spiritual goals aligned with God's will.

• Staying focused on Christ amidst distractions.

• Living out one's faith through service, love, and obedience.

Chapter 4: Overcoming Obstacles on the Track

Every runner faces challenges, and this chapter addresses common struggles that Christians encounter during their spiritual journey. Topics include:

• Dealing with doubt, fear, and discouragement (referencing **Isaiah 41:10**).

• Resisting temptation using strategies from **James 4:7**.

• Trusting in God's strength when facing trials **(2 Corinthians 12:9)**.

Chapter 5: Encouragement from Fellow Runners

In this chapter, Apostle Amor highlights the importance of community in running the race. Drawing from verses like **Hebrews 10:24-25**, it explores:

• The role of fellowship in encouraging perseverance.

• Learning from biblical figures who ran their races faithfully (e.g., Paul, Moses).

• Supporting others in their spiritual journeys.

Chapter 6: Staying Focused on the Finish Line

This chapter reminds readers to keep their eyes fixed on Jesus Christ, who is both the author and finisher of their faith (**Hebrews 12:1-2**). It includes:

• Maintaining an eternal perspective amid worldly distractions.

• Trusting God's promises about heavenly rewards (**Revelation 22:12**).

• Finding joy in knowing that finishing well glorifies God.

Chapter 7: The Eternal Prize – Finishing Strong

The final chapter ties everything together by focusing on what it means to finish strong. Using Scriptures like **2 Timothy 4:7**, I encourage readers to reflect on their legacy of faith. Key points include:

• Understanding what it means to hear "Well done, good and faithful servant" (**Matthew 25:21**).

• Celebrating victories along the way while keeping eternity in mind.

• Encouraging others to join you at the finish line.

Additional Features

To enhance reader engagement and provide practical application, each chapter includes:

1. Reflection Questions – To help readers internalize key lessons.

2. Action Steps – Practical ways to apply biblical principles discussed in each chapter.

3. Inspirational Stories – Testimonies or anecdotes illustrating perseverance in faith.

Conclusion

The book concludes by summarizing its core message—encouraging believers to remain steadfast in their spiritual race—and offering a final word of hope rooted in Scripture.

By structuring his book around these chapters, I provide readers with a comprehensive guide that not only inspires but also equips them to "finish the race" faithfully.

3.   **Living with an Eternal Perspective**

To run effectively toward eternal prizes requires adopting an eternal perspective—viewing daily decisions through the lens of eternity rather than immediate gratification or worldly success.

Chapter 1: Understanding the Spiritual Race

Life is often presented in Scripture as a journey, a pilgrimage, or, significantly, **a race**. This metaphor is powerfully articulated in **1 Corinthians 9:24-27**, where the Apostle Paul urges believers to "run in such a way as to get the prize." This passage forms the **biblical basis for viewing life as a race**, emphasizing the need for discipline, focus, and a clear objective in the Christian walk. The imagery of an athletic competition, familiar to the Corinthians, served to illustrate the earnestness and effort required in pursuing God's calling.

Recognizing **God's calling** is paramount in this spiritual race. It's not merely about activity, but about purposeful activity aligned with divine will. Just as a runner trains for a specific event, Christians are called to live in accordance with the unique purpose God has for them, which often involves serving others and spreading the Gospel. This calling differentiates the Christian race from a general pursuit of success, grounding it in a divine mandate rather than personal ambition. The ultimate distinction lies in the nature of the rewards. While earthly races offer perishable crowns and fleeting glory, the spiritual race promises **eternal prizes**—an imperishable crown and an enduring inheritance in Christ. This contrast highlights the superior value of spiritual pursuits over worldly achievements, urging believers to invest in what has lasting significance.

The biblical basis for viewing life as a race is rooted in numerous passages that draw parallels between the Christian life and athletic competitions, emphasizing themes of effort, self-denial, perseverance, and a defined goal. This metaphor is frequently employed by the Apostle Paul in his writings.

The Christian life is often depicted as a **marathon, not a sprint**, requiring sustained effort and a long-term perspective rather than immediate, dramatic results. This imagery highlights the need for continuous, incremental progress towards spiritual maturity. Key biblical figures like Paul, Caleb, and Daniel are presented as examples of those who finished their spiritual race well, while others like King Saul and Samson serve as cautionary tales of those who did not.

Several biblical lessons emerge from this race analogy:

Running to Win: Christians are encouraged to run with the intention of winning the prize, not merely to participate. This "winning" is not about competing against other believers but against "the world, the flesh, and the devil". The prize is an "imperishable wreath" and the joy of eternal fellowship with Christ.

Avoiding Distractions and Staying on Track: The race requires focus and avoiding anything that might hinder progress, such as poor choices in companions or looking back at past failures. Paul emphasizes "forgetting what lies behind and reaching forward to what lies ahead".

Endurance and Perseverance: The Christian race is a lifelong endeavor that demands endurance through trials, tragedies, and suffering. It's about consistently obeying God and keeping one's eyes fixed on Jesus, who is the "author and finisher of our faith".

Self-Control and Discipline: Athletes exercise self-control in all things to achieve their perishable prize; similarly, Christians are called to discipline their bodies and desires to attain an imperishable reward. This discipline extends to all aspects of life, including spiritual practices like Bible study, prayer, and evangelism, as well as managing time, desires, and seeking God's will.

The Finish Line and Reward: The ultimate goal is to finish the race with joy and receive the heavenly prize, which includes hearing "well done" from Jesus and receiving a "crown of righteousness". This perspective provides hope and motivation, reminding believers that God, who began a good work in them, will bring it to completion.

In Philippians 3:8, the Apostle Paul asserts that **everything he once valued is now considered "loss" and "rubbish" when compared to the surpassing worth of knowing Christ Jesus as his Lord**. This statement reflects a radical re-evaluation of priorities, where worldly achievements, status, and even religious credentials become insignificant in light of an intimate, personal relationship with Jesus Christ.

Paul's perspective is rooted in his own transformative experience. Prior to his conversion, he was a zealous Pharisee, boasting in his pedigree (circumcised on the eighth day, of the people of Israel, of the tribe of Benjamin, a Hebrew of Hebrews) and his performance under the law (a Pharisee, a persecutor of the church, blameless as to righteousness under the law). These were considered significant "gains" in his former life. However, upon encountering Christ, these former gains were reclassified as "loss".

The term "rubbish" (Greek: skubalon) used by Paul is a strong and vivid word, often translated as "dung," "garbage," or "refuse". This deliberate choice of language emphasizes the utter worthlessness of these things in comparison to Christ. It's not that these things are inherently evil, but rather that their value pales in comparison to the infinite worth of knowing Jesus. This concept is akin to the parables of the hidden treasure and the pearl of great price, where a person sells everything they own to acquire something of immeasurable value.

The "knowing Christ" Paul refers to is not merely intellectual understanding, but a deep, experiential, and relational knowledge. It signifies an intimate union and personal devotion to Jesus as Lord. This pursuit of Christ involves prioritizing Him above all else, even if it means suffering the loss of worldly possessions, reputation, or comfort. Paul's ultimate goal in counting all things as loss is to "gain Christ" and "be found in Him," relying on God's righteousness through faith rather than his own efforts. This radical shift in values underscores the transformative power of a relationship with Christ, where everything else becomes secondary to Him.

Recognizing God's calling is of paramount importance for several profound reasons, impacting an individual's purpose, fulfillment, and eternal trajectory.

Firstly, **it provides a clear sense of purpose and direction in life**. Without understanding one's divine calling, life can feel aimless, leading to confusion and a lack of motivation. God's calling gives meaning to daily activities, transforming mundane tasks into opportunities to serve a higher purpose. It helps individuals align their gifts, talents, and passions with God's will, leading to a more focused and intentional existence.

Secondly, **it leads to genuine fulfillment and deep satisfaction**. When individuals operate within God's intended purpose for their lives, they experience a profound sense of peace and contentment that worldly achievements often fail to provide. This fulfillment is not dependent on external circumstances but stems from an inner conviction that one is living in accordance with divine design. Disregarding or missing God's calling can lead to a persistent feeling of emptiness or dissatisfaction, even amidst apparent success.

Thirdly, **it enables individuals to make a significant impact on the world and in the Kingdom of God**. Every calling, whether it's in ministry, business, arts, education, or family life, is designed to contribute to God's redemptive plan. Recognizing and embracing this calling empowers believers to use their unique abilities to bless others, spread the Gospel, and bring about positive change in their spheres of influence. It transforms ordinary lives into instruments of God's extraordinary work.

Fourthly, **it fosters a deeper relationship with God**. The process of discerning and pursuing God's calling requires constant communication, reliance, and obedience to Him. This journey strengthens faith, builds trust, and cultivates a more intimate walk with the Creator. It teaches individuals to listen to His voice, follow His leading, and depend on His strength, rather than their own.

Finally, **it ensures that one's life investment yields eternal rewards**. The Bible teaches that actions done in obedience to God's calling have eternal significance and will be rewarded. Living out one's calling means investing in things that last beyond this earthly life, contributing to God's eternal Kingdom. Conversely, a life lived outside of God's calling, no matter how successful by worldly standards, may ultimately prove to be unfruitful in an eternal context.

In essence, recognizing God's calling is not merely about finding a job or a role; it's about discovering one's true identity and purpose within God's grand narrative, leading to a life of profound meaning, lasting impact, and eternal significance.

Differentiating between earthly rewards and eternal prizes is a fundamental concept in Christian theology, highlighting the contrasting values and lasting significance of what one pursues in life.

Earthly rewards are those benefits, accolades, and possessions that are gained in this present life. They are temporary, perishable, and ultimately cannot be taken beyond the grave. Examples include wealth, fame, power, material possessions, human approval, and worldly success. While not inherently evil, an excessive focus on earthly rewards can lead to a neglect of spiritual priorities and a misplaced sense of security. Jesus himself warned against storing up treasures on earth, "where moths and vermin destroy, and where thieves break in and steal" (Matthew 6:19). The pursuit of earthly rewards often involves striving for recognition, comfort, and immediate gratification.

In contrast, **eternal prizes** are the spiritual blessings, commendations, and rewards that are bestowed by God in the afterlife, specifically in heaven. These prizes are imperishable, incorruptible, and have lasting value beyond this earthly existence. They are often described as

"crowns" in the New Testament, such as the crown of righteousness (2 Timothy 4:8), the crown of life (James 1:12; Revelation 2:10), the crown of glory (1 Peter 5:4), and the imperishable crown (1 Corinthians 9:25). These prizes are not earned through human merit but are gracious rewards from God for faithful service, perseverance in trials, and living a life dedicated to His will. The focus is on spiritual growth, obedience, self-sacrifice, and investing in God's kingdom. The ultimate eternal prize is often considered to be the joy of being in God's presence and hearing His commendation, "Well done, good and faithful servant" (Matthew 25:21). The distinction emphasizes that while earthly rewards are fleeting, eternal prizes are enduring and represent true spiritual wealth.

Run to Jesus. Always follow Him.

1 John 2:15

Do not love the world or the things in the world.

If anyone loves the world, the love of the Father is not in him.

John 8:23

And He said to them, "You are from beneath; I am from above. You are of this world; I am not of this world."

John 17:9

I pray for them: I pray not for the world, but for them which thou hast given me; for they are thine.

Matt 15:13

But He answered and said, "Every plant which My heavenly Father has not planted will be uprooted. 14Let them alone. They are blind leaders of the blind. And if the blind leads the blind, both will fall into a ditch."

Conclusion

Understanding life as a spiritual race transforms how believers approach their faith journey. By grounding themselves in Scripture's teachings about purposefulness (1 Corinthians 9), recognizing God's unique calling upon them (Ephesians 2), and prioritizing eternal rewards over temporary gains (Matthew 6), Christians can begin running their races with clarity and conviction.

This foundational understanding sets up subsequent chapters where we'll explore practical strategies for overcoming obstacles along this spiritual path while remaining focused on finishing well—for only those who endure until completion receive what truly matters most: everlasting fellowship with our Creator!

Chapter 2: Preparing for the Journey

Preparation is essential for any race, and the spiritual race of faith is no exception. Just as an athlete would never step onto the track without proper training, equipment, and focus, believers must also prepare themselves spiritually to run well and finish strong. This chapter delves into how Christians can equip themselves for their journey of faith by building a strong foundation in God, utilizing spiritual tools, and cultivating discipline.

Building a Strong Relationship with God

The first step in preparing for the spiritual race is establishing and maintaining a deep relationship with God. This connection serves as the foundation upon which all other preparation is built. Without it, believers risk running aimlessly or losing sight of their ultimate goal.

1. **Prayer as Communication with God**

Prayer is not merely a ritual but an ongoing conversation with God that strengthens our bond with Him. Through prayer, believers seek guidance, express gratitude, confess sins, and intercede for others. As Ephesians 6:18 states:

"With all prayer and petition pray [with specific requests] at all times [on every occasion and in every season] in the Spirit..." (AMP).

Apostle Amor emphasizes that consistent prayer aligns our hearts with God's will and provides us with the strength to face life's challenges.

2. **Scripture Study as Spiritual Nourishment**

Just as athletes need proper nutrition to fuel their bodies, Christians require spiritual nourishment through studying

God's Word. The Bible serves as both a guidebook and a source of encouragement for those running the race of faith. Psalm 119:105 declares:

"Your word is a lamp to my feet and a light to my path" (AMP).

By meditating on scripture daily, believers gain wisdom, clarity, and direction for their journey.

Equipping Oneself with Spiritual Tools

In Ephesians 6:10-18, Paul describes the "Armor of God," which equips believers to stand firm against spiritual opposition. Apostle Amor highlights this passage as essential preparation for anyone embarking on their faith journey:

1. The Belt of Truth

Truth is foundational in combating deception from the enemy or worldly influences. Knowing God's truth allows believers to discern right from wrong and remain steadfast in their convictions.

2. The Breastplate of Righteousness

Righteousness protects our hearts from sin's corrupting influence. Living righteously means striving to align our actions with God's standards.

3. The Shield of Faith

Faith acts as a shield against doubt and fear—two common obstacles in the spiritual race. Hebrews 11:1 reminds us that faith is "the assurance [title deed] of things hoped for" (AMP), enabling us to trust God's promises even when circumstances seem uncertain.

4. The Helmet of Salvation

Salvation guards our minds against despair or hopelessness by reminding us of Christ's redemptive work on the cross.

5. The Sword of the Spirit (God's Word)

The Word of God serves as both an offensive weapon against lies and a source of encouragement during trials.

By putting on this armor daily through prayerful reflection and intentional living, believers are better equipped to face challenges along their journey

Developing Discipline and Self-Control

No athlete achieves success without discipline—and neither can Christians expect to run their spiritual race effectively without self-control. In 1 Corinthians 9:25-27 (AMP), Paul writes:

"Now every athlete who goes into training conducts himself temperately and restricts himself in all things... I discipline my body [like an athlete], making it my slave..."

I draw three key lessons from this passage:

1. Consistency Matters

Just as athletes train regularly to build endurance, Christians must consistently engage in practices like prayer, worship, fellowship, and service to grow spiritually.

2. Sacrifice Is Necessary

Discipline often requires giving up certain comforts or distractions that hinder progress—whether it's excessive entertainment or unhealthy habits—in order to prioritize time with God.

3. Focus on Eternal Rewards

Unlike earthly competitions where prizes are temporary

(e.g., trophies or medals), Paul reminds us that the reward for faithful living is eternal life with Christ—a prize worth every sacrifice made along the way (1 Corinthians 9:25).

Conclusion

Preparing for the journey requires intentional effort on multiple fronts—building a strong relationship with God through prayer and scripture study; equipping oneself with spiritual tools like truth, righteousness, faith; and developing discipline rooted in self-control. Apostle Amor encourages readers not only to prepare but also to remain vigilant throughout their race so they may finish well and receive their eternal reward.

As Philippians 3:14 (AMP) beautifully states:

"I press on toward the goal to win the [heavenly] prize of the upward call of God in Christ Jesus."

By following these principles outlined in Scripture—and applying them diligently, believers can confidently embark on their journey knowing they are fully prepared for whatever lies ahead.

Chapter 3: Running with Purpose

The Christian life is often compared to a race, not one of speed but of endurance, focus, and intentionality. In this chapter, we will explore what it means to run with purpose in the spiritual race. Drawing from Scripture and real-life testimonies, we will examine how believers can set spiritual goals aligned with God's will, stay focused on Christ amidst distractions, and live out their faith through service, love, and obedience.

Setting Spiritual Goals Aligned with God's Will

One of the most important aspects of running with purpose is having a clear sense of direction. Just as athletes train with specific goals in mind—whether it's completing a marathon or breaking a personal record—Christians must also set spiritual goals that align with God's will for their lives. The Apostle Paul provides a powerful example of this in **Philippians 3:13-14**:

"Brothers and sisters, I do not consider that I have made it my own yet; but one thing I do: forgetting what lies behind and reaching forward to what lies ahead, I press on toward the goal to win the [heavenly] prize of the upward call of God in Christ Jesus."

Paul's words remind us that our ultimate goal is not earthly success or recognition but the "heavenly prize"—eternal life with Christ. To run with purpose, believers must first seek God's guidance through prayer and scripture study to discern His unique calling for their lives. This might involve pursuing a ministry role, serving others in practical ways, or simply growing deeper in personal holiness.

Real-life testimony: Consider Sarah, a young woman who

felt called to start a community outreach program for under-privileged youth. Through prayer and careful planning, she set clear goals for her ministry: providing mentorship opportunities, organizing educational workshops, and sharing the gospel message. By aligning her efforts with God's will, Sarah was able to make a lasting impact on her community while staying focused on her ultimate goal—glorifying Christ.

Staying Focused on Christ Amidst Distractions

Running with purpose also requires unwavering focus. In today's world, distractions abound—social media, career pressures, materialism—but Christians are called to fix their eyes on Jesus as their ultimate example and source of strength. The author of Hebrews captures this beautifully in **Hebrews 12:1-2:**

"Therefore, since we are surrounded by so great a cloud of witnesses [who by faith have testified to the truth of God's absolute faithfulness], stripping off every unnecessary weight and the sin which so easily entangles us, let us run with endurance and active persistence the race that is set before us—[looking away from all that will distract us and] focusing our eyes on Jesus..."

To stay focused amidst distractions:

• Regularly spend time in prayer and worship.

• Meditate on Scripture to renew your mind (Romans 12:2).

• Surround yourself with fellow believers who encourage you in your walk with Christ.

Real-life testimony: John was an ambitious professional who found himself consumed by his career aspirations.

Despite achieving financial success, he felt spiritually empty. After attending a church retreat where he recommitted his life to Christ, John began prioritizing daily devotions and joined a small group for accountability. By shifting his focus back to Jesus, John discovered true fulfillment that no worldly achievement could provide.

Living Out One's Faith Through Service, Love, and Obedience

Finally, running with purpose involves putting faith into action through service, love for others, and obedience to God's commands. James reminds us that faith without works is dead (James 2:26), emphasizing the importance of living out our beliefs in tangible ways.

Jesus Himself modeled this principle when He washed His disciples' feet—a powerful act of humility and service (John 13:12-17). As followers of Christ:

• Serve others selflessly within your family, church community, or workplace.

• Show love even when it's difficult (Matthew 5:44).

• Obey God's Word even when it challenges societal norms or personal preferences.

Real-life testimony: Maria felt convicted during a sermon about loving her neighbors as herself (Mark 12:31). She decided to volunteer at a local homeless shelter every weekend despite her busy schedule. Over time, Maria built meaningful relationships with those she served while deepening her own understanding of God's love.

Conclusion

Running with purpose means living intentionally as followers of Christ—setting spiritual goals aligned with His will; staying focused on Him amidst life's distractions; and actively demonstrating our faith through service, love, and obedience. As we press on toward the heavenly prize promised by Scripture (Philippians 3:14), let us remember that our strength comes not from ourselves but from the One who has already secured victory on our behalf.

Chapter 4: Overcoming Obstacles on the Track

Every runner, whether in a physical race or the spiritual journey of life, encounters obstacles that test their endurance, resolve, and focus. These challenges are inevitable but not insurmountable. In this chapter, we will explore how Christians can overcome common struggles such as doubt, fear, discouragement, temptation, and trials by relying on God's Word and His promises. Drawing from key biblical passages, we will uncover practical strategies to help believers stay steadfast and finish their race with faith.

Dealing with Doubt, Fear, and Discouragement

One of the most pervasive obstacles Christians face is doubt—doubt about their purpose, God's plan for their lives, or even His presence during difficult times. Fear often accompanies doubt, creating a sense of paralysis that prevents believers from moving forward in their spiritual journey. Discouragement can follow when progress feels slow or when setbacks occur.

The Bible provides clear guidance for overcoming these emotions. **Isaiah 41:10** offers a powerful reminder of God's unwavering support:

"Do not fear [anything], for I am with you; Do not be afraid, for I am your God. I will strengthen you; be assured I will help you;I will certainly take hold of you with My righteous right hand [a hand of justice, of power, of victory, of salvation]." (AMP)

This verse reassures believers that they are never alone in their struggles. God promises His presence ("I am with you"), His strength ("I will strengthen you"), and His active intervention ("I will help you"). To combat doubt and fear:

1. **Meditate on Scripture**: Memorize verses like Isaiah 41:10 to remind yourself of God's promises during moments of uncertainty.

2. **Pray Honestly**: Bring your doubts and fears before God in prayer. He invites us to cast all our anxieties on Him because He cares for us (1 Peter 5:7).

3. **Seek Encouragement from Fellow Believers**: Surround yourself with a supportive community that can uplift you through prayer and encouragement.

Resisting Temptation

Temptation is another significant hurdle on the spiritual track. It seeks to divert believers from their path by appealing to worldly desires or offering shortcuts that compromise integrity and faithfulness to God.

The Bible provides a clear strategy for resisting temptation in **James 4:7**:

"So submit to [the authority of] God. Resist the devil [stand firm against him], and he will flee from you." (AMP)

This verse outlines two critical steps:

1. **Submit to God**: Align your heart and actions with His will by surrendering every area of your life to Him.

2. **Resist the Devil**: Actively oppose temptation by standing firm in your faith.

Practical ways to resist temptation include:

• **Prayer**: Jesus taught His disciples to pray for deliverance from temptation (Matthew 6:13). Regular prayer strengthens your connection with God and equips you to face challenges.

• **Scripture Study**: When Jesus was tempted in the wilderness (Matthew 4), He countered each temptation with Scripture. Knowing God's Word enables you to recognize lies and respond with truth.

• **Accountability**: Share your struggles with trusted Christian friends or mentors who can provide guidance and hold you accountable.

Remember that resisting temptation is not about relying solely on your own strength but about leaning into God's power through submission and faith.

Trusting in God's Strength During Trials

Trials are an inevitable part of life's race—they test our endurance and refine our character (James 1:2-4). However, they can also feel overwhelming if we rely solely on our own abilities to overcome them.

In **2 Corinthians 12:9**, Paul shares a profound truth he learned during his own trials:

"But He has said to me, 'My grace is sufficient for you [My lovingkindness and My mercy are more than enough—always available—regardless of the situation]; for My power is being perfected [and is completed and shows itself most effectively] in [your] weakness.' Therefore, I will all the more gladly boast in my weaknesses, so that the power of Christ may completely enfold me and may dwell in me." (AMP)

This passage reveals three key principles:

1. **God's Grace Is Sufficient**: No matter how difficult the trial may seem, God's grace provides everything we need to endure it.

2. **God's Power Is Perfected in Weakness**: Our limitations create opportunities for God's strength to shine through.

3. **Boast in Weaknesses**: Instead of hiding or resenting our weaknesses, we should embrace them as opportunities for Christ's power to work within us.

To trust in God's strength during trials:

• **Acknowledge Your Dependence on Him**: Admit that you cannot navigate challenges alone and invite Him into your situation.

• **Focus on His Promises**: Reflect on verses like Romans 8:28 ("And we know [with great confidence] that God [who is deeply concerned about us] causes all things to work together [as a plan] for good...").

• **Rejoice Despite Circumstances**: Like Paul did while imprisoned (Philippians 4), choose joy even amid hardship as an act of faith.

Conclusion

Overcoming obstacles on the spiritual track requires intentionality, perseverance, and reliance on God's Word. Whether dealing with doubt, resisting temptation, or enduring trials:

• Remember Isaiah 41:10 when fear arises—God is always present.

• Apply James 4:7 when faced with temptation—submit fully to God while resisting evil.

• Lean into 2 Corinthians 12:9 during trials—God's grace is sufficient even when we feel weak.

By trusting in God's promises and equipping ourselves with biblical strategies, we can overcome any obstacle that threatens our progress toward finishing the race set before us.

Chapter 5: Encouragement from Fellow Runners

In this chapter, I will delve into the vital role of community and fellowship in the spiritual race. Drawing inspiration from Hebrews 10:24-25, which urges believers to "consider how we may spur one another on toward love and good deeds" and to "not give up meeting together," I emphasize that no one is meant to run the race of faith alone. The chapter highlights three key aspects of encouragement from fellow runners: the power of fellowship, lessons from biblical figures, and the importance of supporting others in their spiritual journeys.

The Role of Fellowship in Encouraging Perseverance

I begin by stressing that fellowship is a cornerstone of Christian life. Just as athletes benefit from training alongside teammates who push them to excel, Christians are strengthened when they surround themselves with other believers. Fellowship provides accountability, motivation, and emotional support during challenging times.

Hebrews 10:24-25 serves as the foundation for this discussion. I will unpack these verses by explaining how gathering with other believers fosters an environment where individuals can encourage one another to remain steadfast in their faith. Scripture says:

"When we come together as a community of believers, we remind each other of God's promises and help carry each other's burdens (Galatians 6:2). This shared journey strengthens us to keep running even when the path feels difficult."

The chapter also explores practical ways to cultivate meaningful fellowship, such as participating in small groups, attending church regularly, and engaging in acts of service together. I encourage readers to seek out relationships that challenge them spiritually and help them grow closer to God.

Learning from Biblical Figures Who Ran Their Races Faithfully

Next, we turn to examples from Scripture to illustrate how faithful runners have navigated their spiritual races. Let's highlight several biblical figures whose lives serve as powerful testimonies of perseverance:

1. **Paul** - The apostle Paul is presented as a model of unwavering commitment despite immense trials. From imprisonment to persecution, Paul remained focused on his mission to spread the Gospel (2 Timothy 4:7). Apostle Amor reflects on Paul's declaration: *"I have fought the good fight, I have finished the race, I have kept the faith."* This statement inspires readers to stay committed regardless of obstacles.

2. **Moses** - Moses' leadership journey is another example explored in this chapter. Despite facing resistance from Pharaoh, complaints from the Israelites, and personal doubts about his abilities, Moses trusted God's guidance and fulfilled his calling (Exodus 3-14). His story reminds readers that reliance on God equips them for any challenge.

3. **Ruth** - Ruth's loyalty and faithfulness are highlighted as an example of steadfastness in relationships and trust in God's plan (Ruth 1:16-17). Her story demonstrates how perseverance often leads to unexpected blessings.

By examining these figures' lives, Apostle Amor encourages readers not only to draw strength from their examples but also to recognize that they are part of a long lineage of faithful runners who have completed their races before them.

Supporting Others in Their Spiritual Journeys

The final section of this chapter focuses on the importance of helping others run their races well. I explain that encouragement is not a one-way street; just as believers receive support from others, they are called to offer it in return.

Drawing again from Hebrews 10:24-25, he writes:

"Encouragement is both a gift we receive and a responsibility we bear. When we cheer on our fellow runners—through prayer, words of affirmation, or acts of kindness—we reflect Christ's love and strengthen the body of Christ."

Some practical suggestions for supporting others spiritually:

• **Pray for One Another**: Regular intercession builds unity within the body of Christ.

• **Offer Words of Affirmation**: Simple expressions like "I'm praying for you" or "God has great plans for your life" can uplift someone who feels weary.

• **Serve Together**: Partnering with others in ministry or outreach creates opportunities for mutual encouragement.

• **Be Present**: Sometimes simply being there for someone during difficult seasons speaks volumes about God's love.

I conclude this section by reminding readers that supporting others not only helps them but also strengthens their own faith journey. As Proverbs 27:17 says: "As iron sharpens iron, so one person sharpens another."

Conclusion

In Chapter 5: *Encouragement from Fellow Runners*, I underscore that while each believer must run their own race, they are never truly alone. Through fellowship with other Christians, learning from biblical examples, and actively supporting others' spiritual journeys, believers can find renewed strength and purpose.

I close with this reflection:

"The race set before us was never meant to be run in isolation. God has placed us within a community so that we may encourage one another toward love and good deeds until we cross the finish line together."

Chapter 6: Staying Focused on the Finish Line

In this chapter, I emphasize the importance of maintaining focus on Jesus Christ, who is described in Hebrews 12:1-2 as "the author and finisher of our faith." The Christian journey is often compared to a race, and just like any runner striving to cross the finish line, believers must keep their eyes fixed on their ultimate goal: eternal life with God. This chapter provides practical guidance and spiritual encouragement for staying focused amid life's distractions and challenges.

Maintaining an Eternal Perspective Amid Worldly Distractions

One of the greatest challenges Christians face is staying focused on their spiritual race while living in a world filled with distractions. Apostle Amor reminds readers that the Bible consistently calls believers to set their minds on things above rather than earthly concerns. Colossians 3:2 states, "Set your mind and keep focused habitually on the things above [the heavenly things], not on things that are on the earth [which have only temporal value]" (AMP).

I will explain that worldly distractions—such as materialism, social pressures, or even personal ambitions—can easily divert attention from God's purpose for our lives. To combat this, I encourage readers to regularly evaluate their priorities through prayer and scripture study. By doing so, they can ensure that their actions align with God's will and remain centered on His eternal promises.

I also highlight the importance of community in maintaining focus. Surrounding oneself with fellow believers who share a commitment to finishing the race well can provide accountability and encouragement during difficult times. Proverbs 27:17 says, "As iron sharpens iron, so one person sharpens another," underscoring the value of Christian fellowship in staying spiritually grounded.

Trusting God's Promises About Heavenly Rewards

I want to draw attention to Revelation 22:12, where Jesus declares, "Behold, I am coming quickly, and My reward is with Me, to give to each one according to the merit of his deeds [earthly works faithfully done]." This verse serves as a powerful reminder that God has promised rewards for those who faithfully complete their spiritual race.

I explain that these rewards are not merely symbolic but represent tangible expressions of God's love and justice. While earthly achievements may fade or lose significance over time, heavenly rewards are eternal and unchanging. I urge readers to trust in these promises as motivation to persevere through trials and remain steadfast in their faith.

To illustrate this point further, I want to share examples from scripture of individuals who trusted in God's promises despite facing immense challenges. For instance:

• Abraham obeyed God's call to leave his homeland because he trusted in the promise of a better future (Hebrews 11:8-10).

• Paul endured persecution and hardship because he was confident in receiving "the crown of righteousness" reserved for those who love Christ's appearing (2 Timothy 4:7-8).

By reflecting on these examples, readers are encouraged to adopt a similar mindset—one that prioritizes eternal rewards over temporary pleasures or comforts.

Finding Joy in Knowing That Finishing Well Glorifies God

I conclude this chapter by reminding readers that finishing their spiritual race well brings glory to God. I reference John 17:4, where Jesus prays to the Father saying, "I have glorified You down here on the earth by completing the work that You gave Me to do." Just as Jesus glorified God by fulfilling His mission on earth, believers can honor Him by remaining faithful until the end.

I emphasize that joy comes from knowing one's efforts contribute to something far greater than personal success or recognition—they bring glory to the Creator Himself. This perspective shifts the focus away from self-centered motivations and toward a deeper sense of purpose rooted in worshiping and serving God.

Practical steps for cultivating this joy include:

1. **Daily Gratitude**: Regularly thanking God for His grace and guidance helps believers stay mindful of His presence throughout their journey.

2. **Celebrating Milestones**: Recognizing small victories along the way reinforces progress toward finishing well.

3. **Sharing Testimonies**: Telling others about how God has worked in one's life not only encourages them but also strengthens personal faith.

Finally, you and I are never alone in the race. Hebrews 12:1 reminds us that we are surrounded by "a great cloud of witnesses"—faithful believers who have gone before us—and Jesus Himself runs alongside us as both our guide and source of strength.

Conclusion

Staying focused on the finish line requires discipline, perseverance, and unwavering trust in God's promises. By maintaining an eternal perspective amid worldly distractions, trusting in heavenly rewards promised by Scripture (Revelation 22:12), and finding joy in glorifying God through faithful living (John 17:4), Christians can confidently run their race with purpose and determination.

I close this chapter with an encouraging reminder from Philippians 3:14 (AMP): "I press on toward the goal to win [the heavenly] prize of the upward call of God in Christ Jesus." With eyes fixed firmly on Jesus—the author and finisher of our faith—believers can rest assured that they will cross the finish line victoriously.

Chapter 7: The Eternal Prize – Finishing Strong

In this final chapter, I bring the journey of "Don't yah Know? Yah MUST finish the Race First!!!" to a powerful conclusion by focusing on the ultimate goal of every believer: finishing strong and receiving the eternal prize. Drawing from key Scriptures and practical insights, I want to take the time to challenge readers to reflect on their spiritual legacy and live with eternity in mind. This chapter serves as both an encouragement and a call to action, reminding Christians that their faith journey is not just about starting well but about persevering to the end.

Understanding What It Means to Hear "Well Done, Good and Faithful Servant"

I begin by exploring one of the most profound rewards mentioned in Scripture: hearing God say, "Well done, good and faithful servant" (Matthew 25:21). These words signify more than just approval—they represent a life lived in alignment with God's will, marked by obedience, faithfulness, and service.

Using the Parable of the Talents as a foundation (Matthew 25:14-30), I want to emphasize that finishing strong requires believers to steward their gifts, time, and opportunities wisely. I often say:

"God has entrusted each of us with unique talents and responsibilities. To hear those words— 'Well done'—is not about perfection but about faithfulness. It's about running your race with integrity and giving your all for His glory."

I encourage readers to evaluate their lives regularly, asking themselves whether they are living in a way that honors God and fulfills His purpose for them.

Celebrating Victories Along the Way While Keeping Eternity in Mind

While the ultimate prize is eternal life with Christ, it's important to celebrate milestones along the spiritual journey. I draw from Paul's words in 2 Timothy 4:7— "I have fought the good fight, I have finished the race, I have kept the faith"—to illustrate how reflecting on past victories can fuel perseverance.

Step into this mindset:

"Every step forward in your walk with Christ is worth celebrating. Whether it's overcoming a personal struggle or leading someone else closer to Jesus, these moments are glimpses of God's kingdom at work in your life."

However, I caution against becoming complacent or losing sight of eternity. Using Philippians 3:13-14 as a guide— where Paul speaks of forgetting what lies behind and pressing on toward the goal, I implore readers to maintain focus on their heavenly calling.

Encouraging Others to Join You at the Finish Line

One of the most inspiring aspects of this chapter for you, I believe, is its emphasis on community. I remind you that the race is not run in isolation; rather, you are called to encourage others along the way. Hebrews 10:24-25 serves as a cornerstone for this message:

"And let us consider how we may spur one another on toward love and good deeds... encouraging one another— and all the more as you see the Day approaching."

I share here practical ways believers can inspire others to join them at the finish line:

1. **Share Your Testimony** – Personal stories of God's faithfulness can motivate others to trust Him.

2. **Mentor Younger Believers** – Investing time in discipleship helps others grow spiritually.

3. **Pray for One Another** – Interceding for fellow believers strengthens bonds within the body of Christ.

I close this section by painting a vivid picture of heaven as described in Revelation 7:9-10—a great multitude from every nation standing before God's throne—and encourage readers to imagine celebrating there with those they've impacted during their earthly race.

Conclusion: Running Toward Eternity

This chapter closes with a heartfelt exhortation for readers to finish strong by keeping their eyes fixed on Jesus (Hebrews 12:1-2). Get used to saying:

"The race we're running isn't easy—it requires discipline, endurance, and unwavering faith—but it's worth it because our prize is eternal. When I cross that finish line into eternity and hear those precious words from our Savior— 'Well done'—I'll know it was all worth it."

I leave you with this final challenge:

"Don't just aim to finish; aim to finish strong. Run your race with everything you've got so that when you stand before God one day, you'll do so without regret."

Conclusion to "Don't yah Know? Yah MUST finish the Race First!!!"

As we come to the end of this journey together, I want to remind you of one vital truth: **you are not running this race alone**. The God who called you into this race is faithful, and He will equip you with everything you need to cross the finish line. The prize awaiting you is not a temporary crown or fleeting glory—it is eternal life in the presence of our Lord and Savior, Jesus Christ. This is the ultimate victory, and it is available to all who run with perseverance and faith.

The race may be long, and at times it may feel overwhelming. But take heart! God's Word assures us that His grace is sufficient for every step of the way (2 Corinthians 12:9). When you stumble, He will lift you up. When you grow weary, He will renew your strength (Isaiah 40:31). And when doubts creep in, remember that your salvation is secure through faith in Jesus Christ.

Now, as we close this book, I want to leave you with a heartfelt prayer—a prayer for assurance, strength, and victory as you run your race toward eternity.

A Prayer for You

Heavenly Father,

I come before You today with a heart full of gratitude for every person reading these words. Thank You for calling them into Your family and setting them on this path of faith. Lord, I pray that You would fill them with an unshakable assurance of their salvation—that they would know beyond a shadow of a doubt that their names are written in the Book of Life.

Father, strengthen them for the race ahead. When challenges arise and obstacles block their path, remind them that You are their refuge and strength, an ever-present help in trouble (Psalm 46:1). Teach them to rely not on their own power but on Your limitless grace and mercy.

Lord Jesus, I ask that You guide their steps so they may run with purpose and endurance. Help them fix their eyes on You—the author and perfecter of our faith—so they do not grow weary or lose heart (Hebrews 12:1-2). Surround them with Your peace that surpasses all understanding and guard their hearts against fear or discouragement.

Holy Spirit, empower them daily to live according to Your Word. Fill them with wisdom to discern Your will and courage to walk in obedience. May they bear fruit that glorifies You and shines as a testimony to others who have yet to join this race.

Finally, Lord, I pray that each reader finishes strong. Let them hear those precious words from You one day: "Well done, good and faithful servant" (Matthew 25:23). May they receive the crown of righteousness reserved for all who long for Your appearing (2 Timothy 4:8).

Thank You for loving us so deeply that You sent Your Son to make this eternal prize possible. We give You all honor, glory, and praise now and forevermore.

In Jesus' mighty name,

Amen.

Beloved reader, as you close this book today but continue your journey tomorrow, remember this: **You are loved by God more than words can express. He has chosen you for such a time as this—to run your race with joy and perseverance until the day you stand before Him victorious.**

Keep running! Keep believing! And never forget—**Yah MUST finish the race first!!!**

With love in Christ,

Apostle Bill Amor

About Apostle Bill Amor

Apostle Bill Amor's life is a testament to the power of faith, perseverance, and divine intervention. Diagnosed with autism as a child and considered high-functioning as an adult, Apostle Amor has faced challenges that would have broken many.

Born into a world that often misunderstood him, young Bill struggled with feelings of isolation and inadequacy. Despite these challenges, he displayed remarkable determination. At the age of 12, he achieved a significant milestone by winning a reading competition—an accomplishment that filled him with pride and optimism. However, this joy was short-lived when his mother tearfully shared devastating news from the doctor: he was not expected to live beyond the age of 28 to 32.

This revelation shattered his world. Overwhelmed by fear and hopelessness, Bill sought solace in his best friend John Straw, only to discover that John had been taken away by his brother Andy. Feeling abandoned and consumed by anger, he fled into the woods near his home. It was there, amidst the trees and shadows of doubt, that he cried out to God in desperation.

Bill's life changed forever on that fateful day. As he climbed a steep hill toward his neighbor's house, he encountered what can only be described as a divine vision: Jesus Christ Himself appeared before him at the top of the hill near a chain-link fence. The image was vivid—Jesus stood before him with pockmarks where His beard had been removed and glistening divots on His cheeks and chin. He did not resemble traditional depictions; instead, He appeared timeless yet distinct from modern trends.

This miraculous encounter marked the beginning of Apostle Amor's transformation. From a young boy who felt lost and unworthy, he grew into a man devoted to spreading God's message of love and repentance. Through trials and tribulations—including struggles with literacy—he found strength in faith and discovered his purpose as an apostle.

Apostle Amor's mission is clear: to guide others toward spiritual healing by sharing his testimony of divine grace. With humility born from hardship and wisdom gained through faith, he invites readers to embark on their own journeys toward repentance and renewal.